US Air Force Coloring Book

Fighter Jets, Combat Planes, Surveillance, Bombers, F-22, F-35, F-15, F-16, B-1, B-52, B-2, A-10, C-17, Cv-22, C-130, Apache & Cobra Helicopters
45 Large Images 8.5" X 11"

Rachel Mintz

This book is not endorsed by the US Air Force

"Aim High... Fly-Fight-Win"

Enjoy 45 coloring pages of US Air Force from missions around the world.

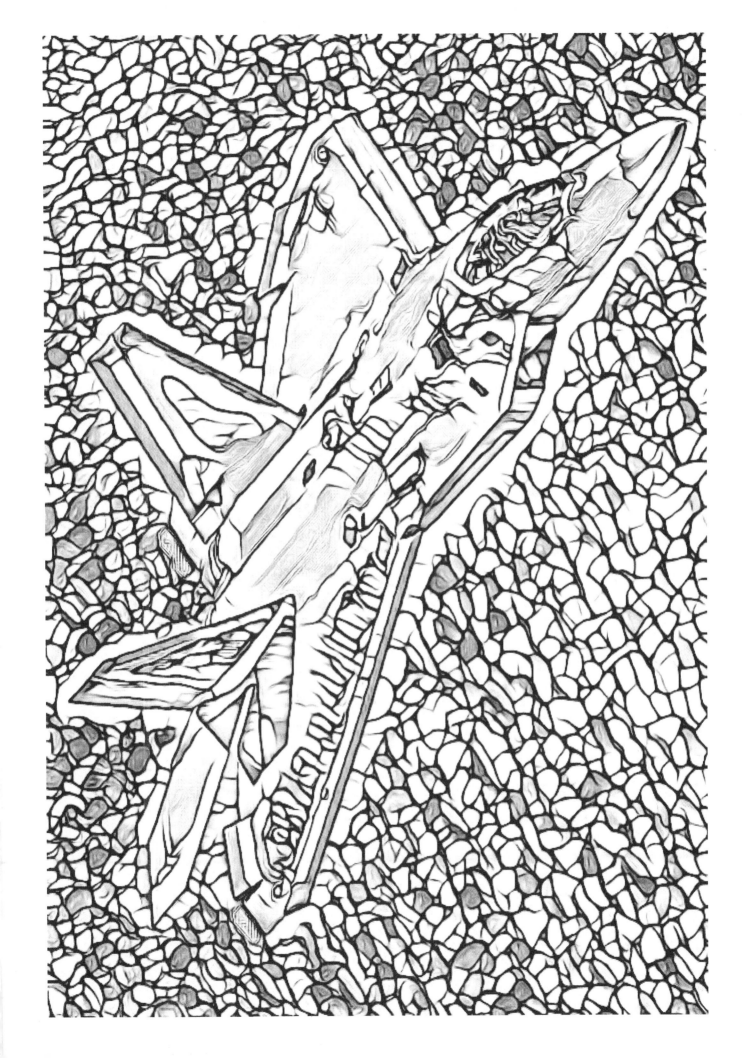

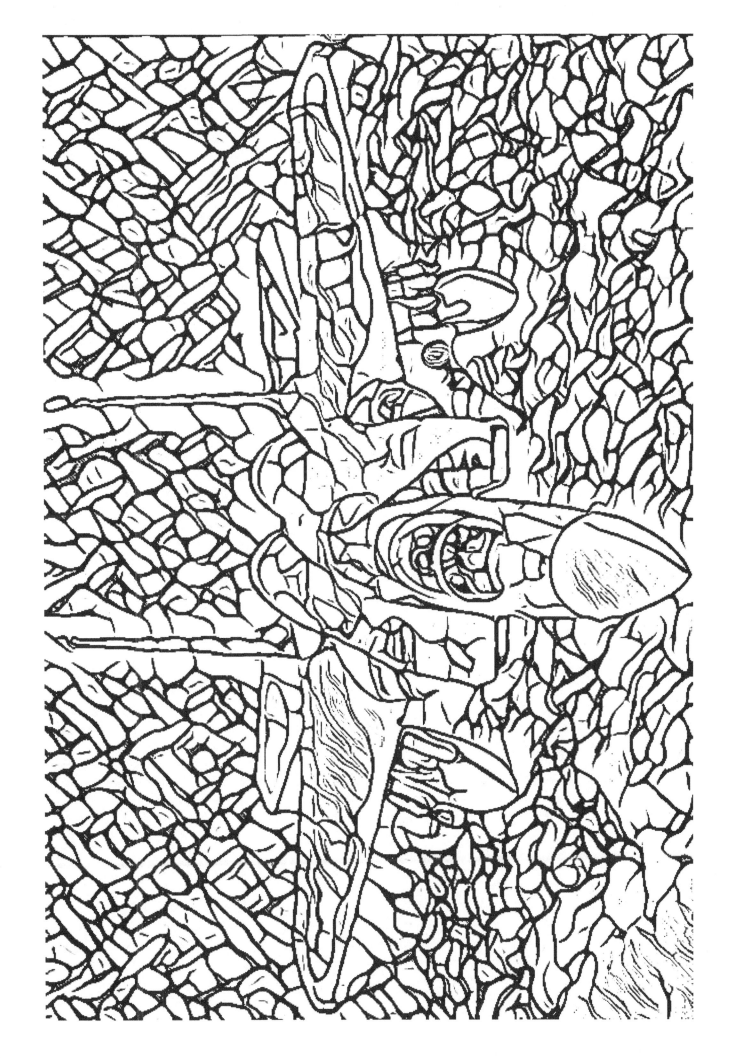

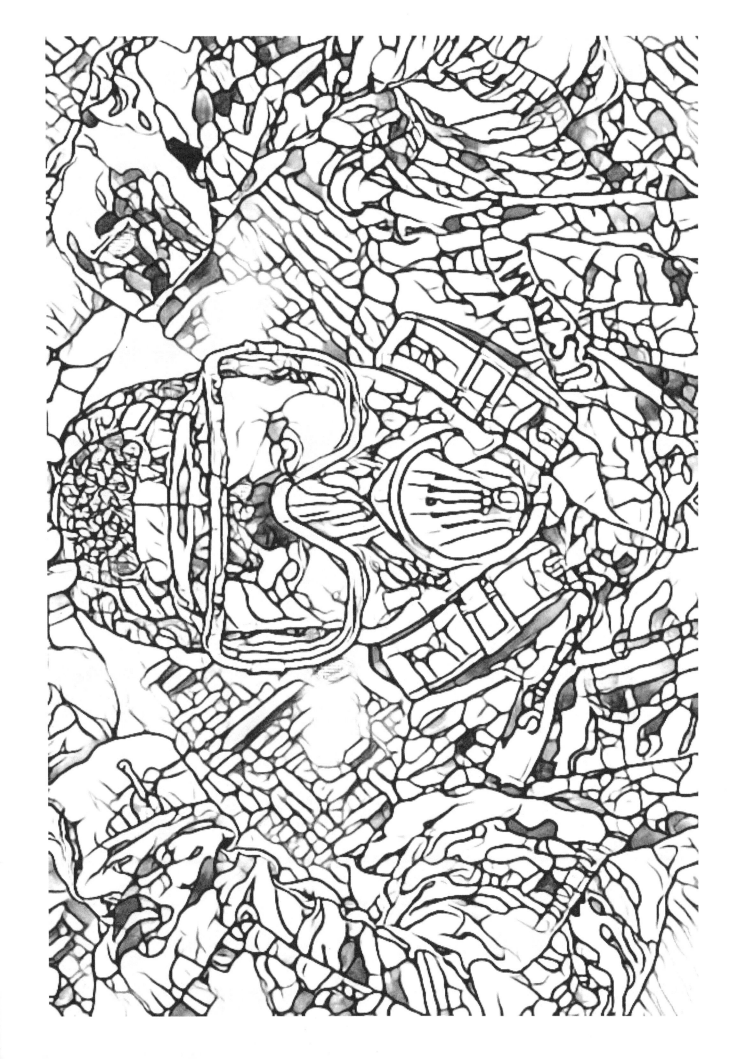

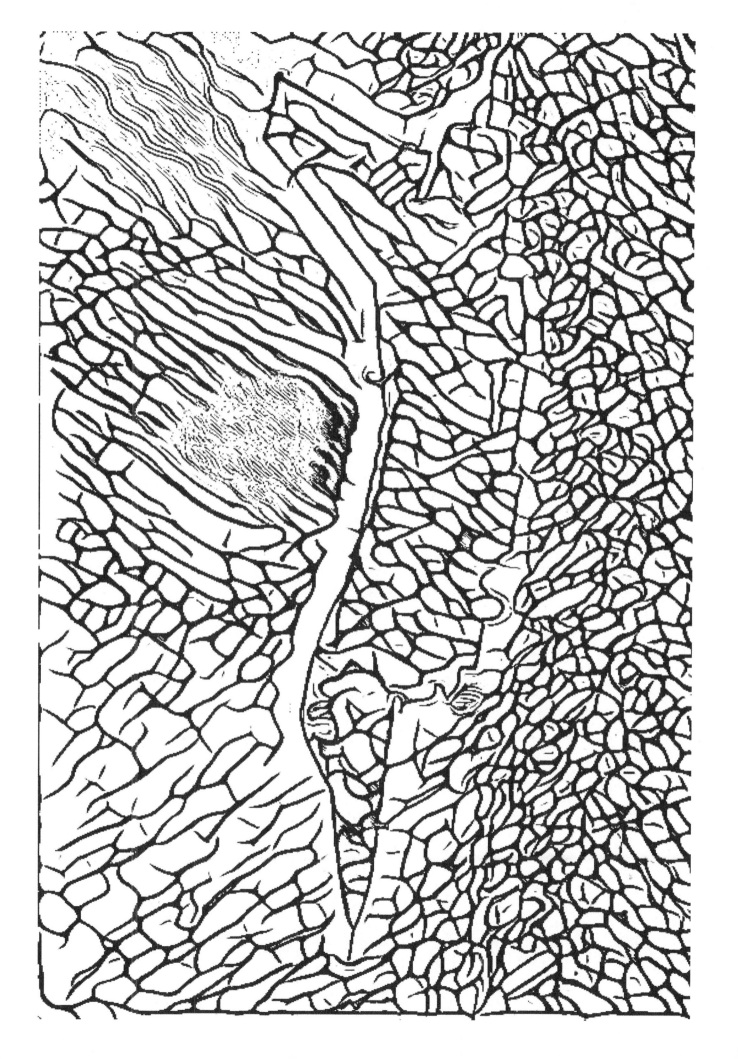

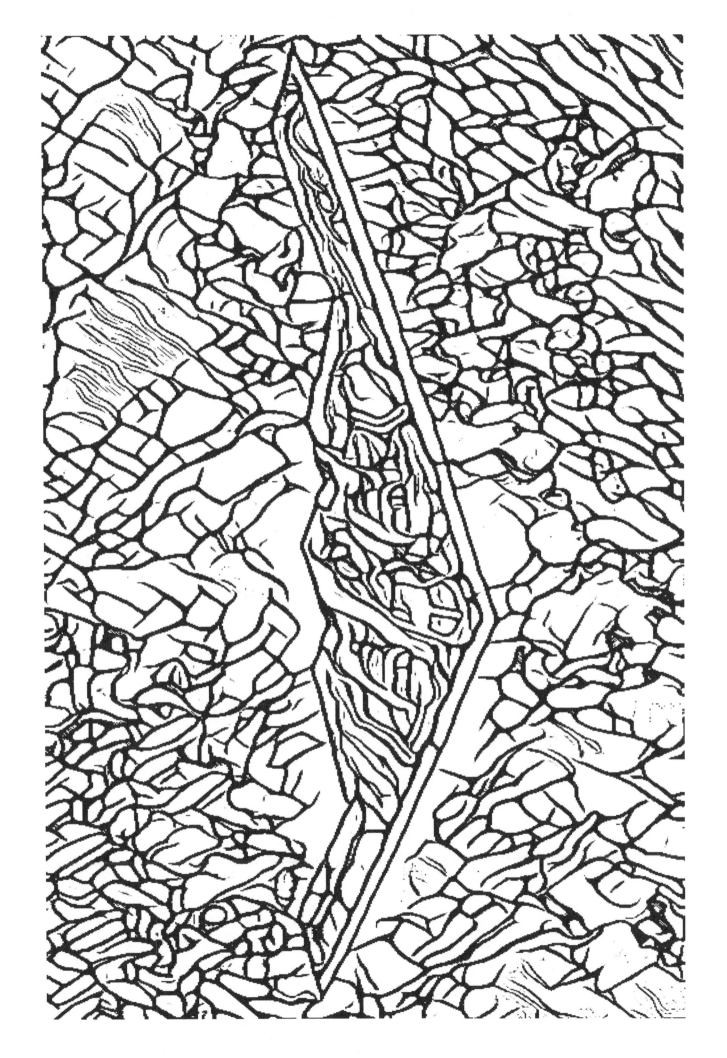

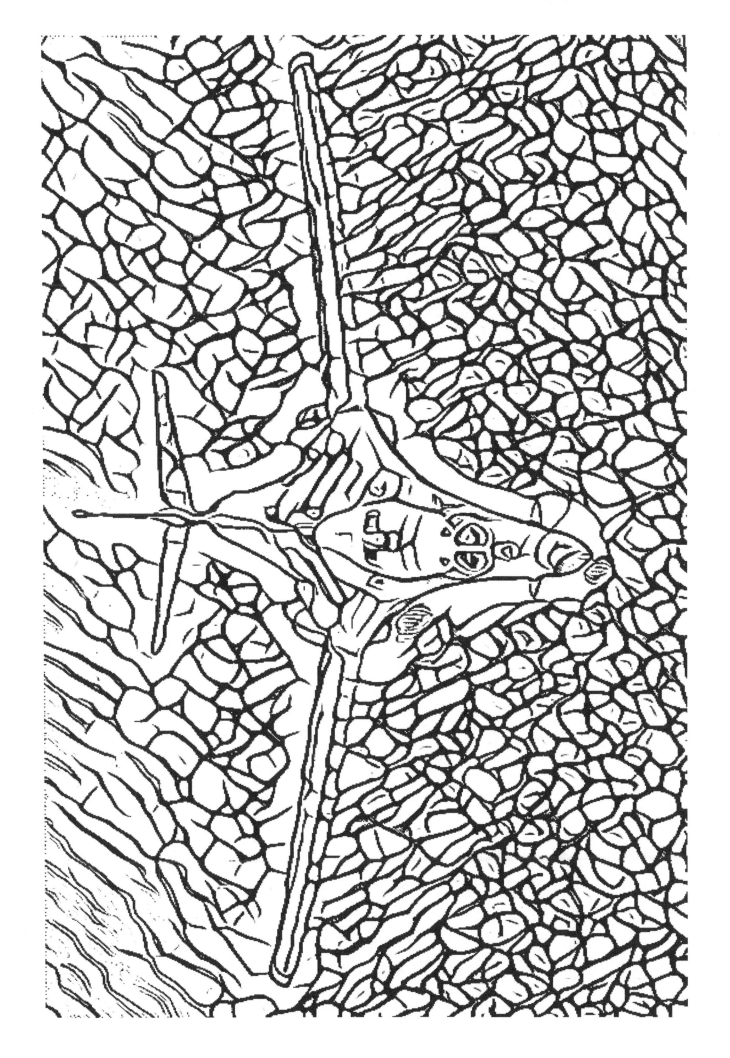

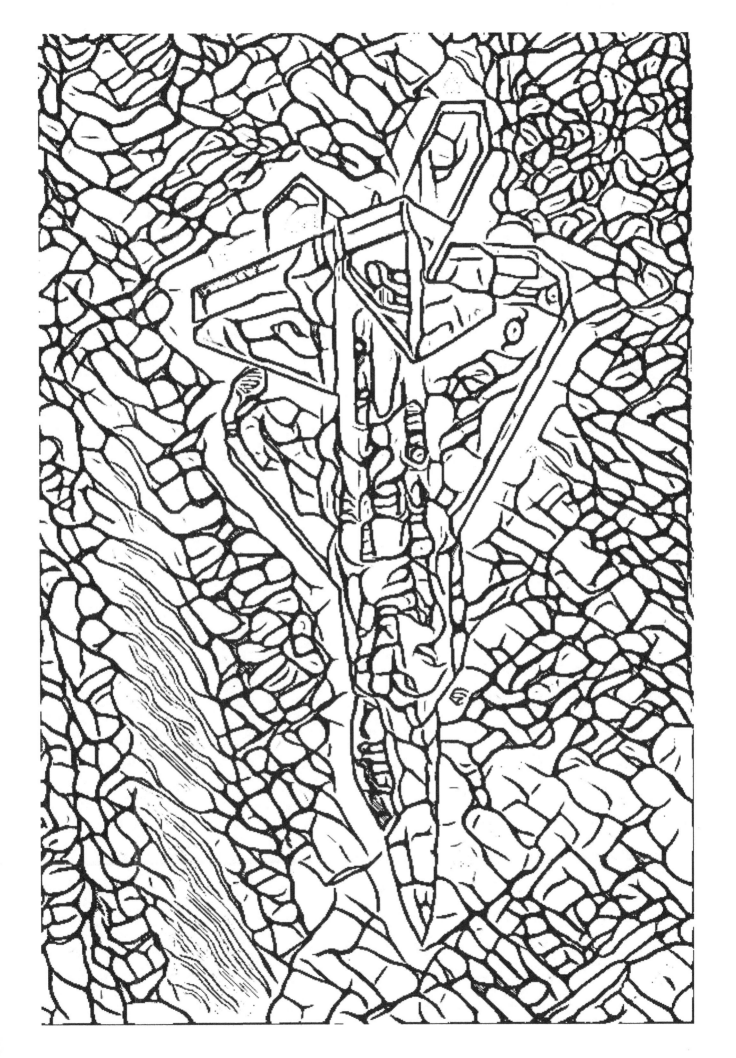

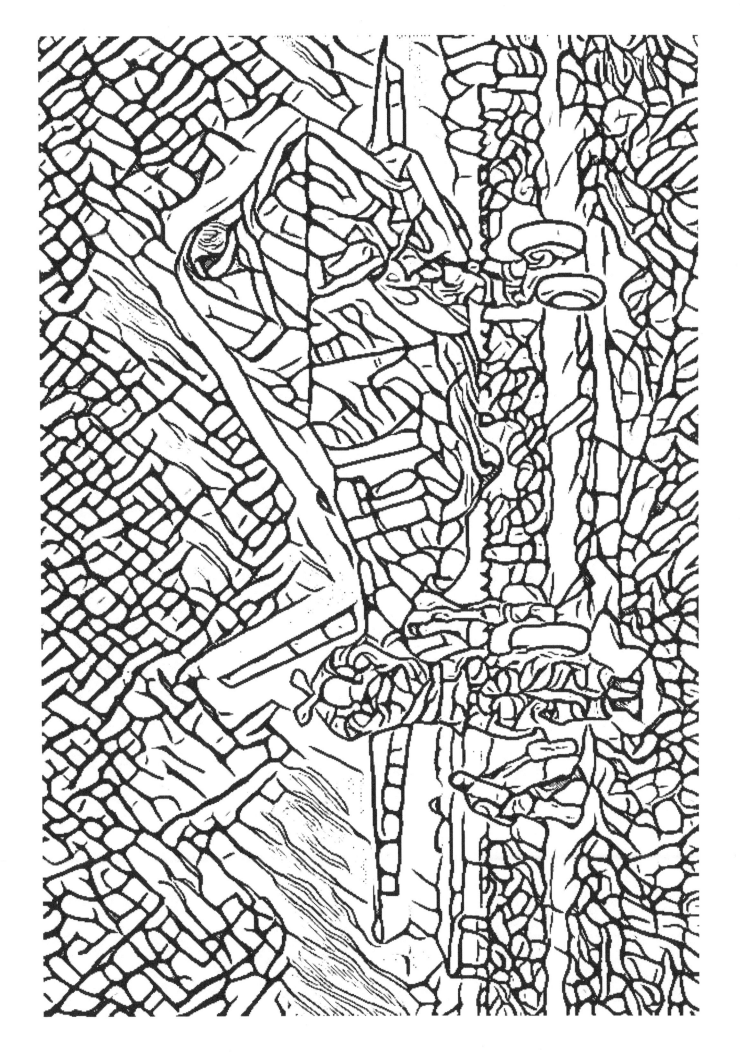

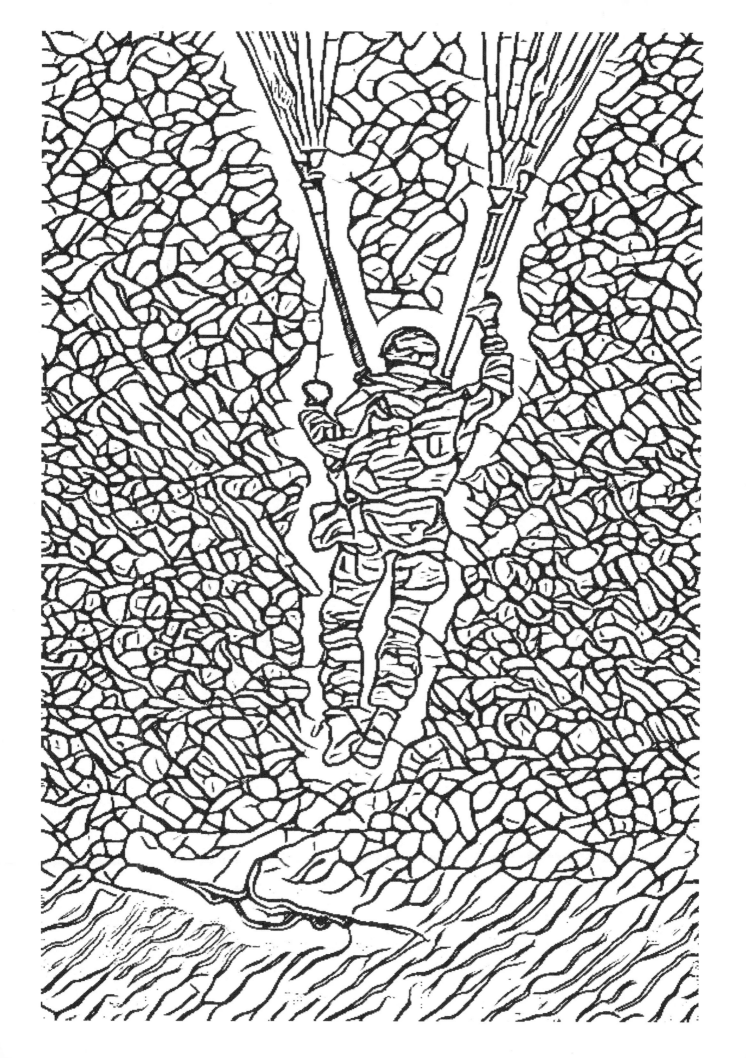

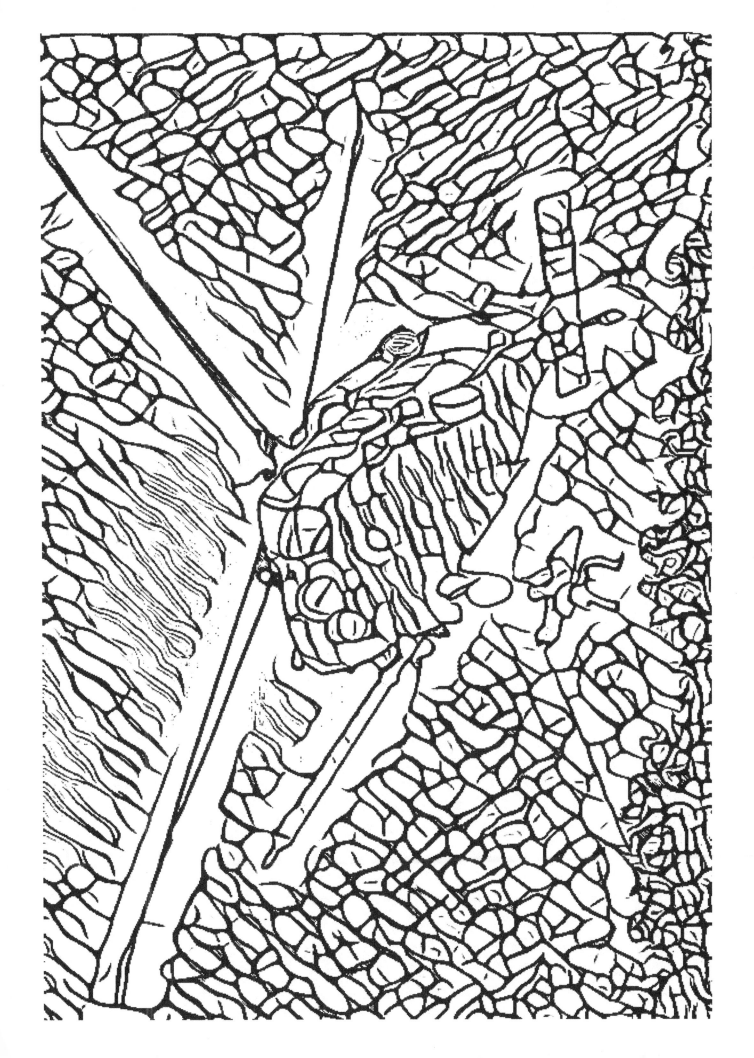

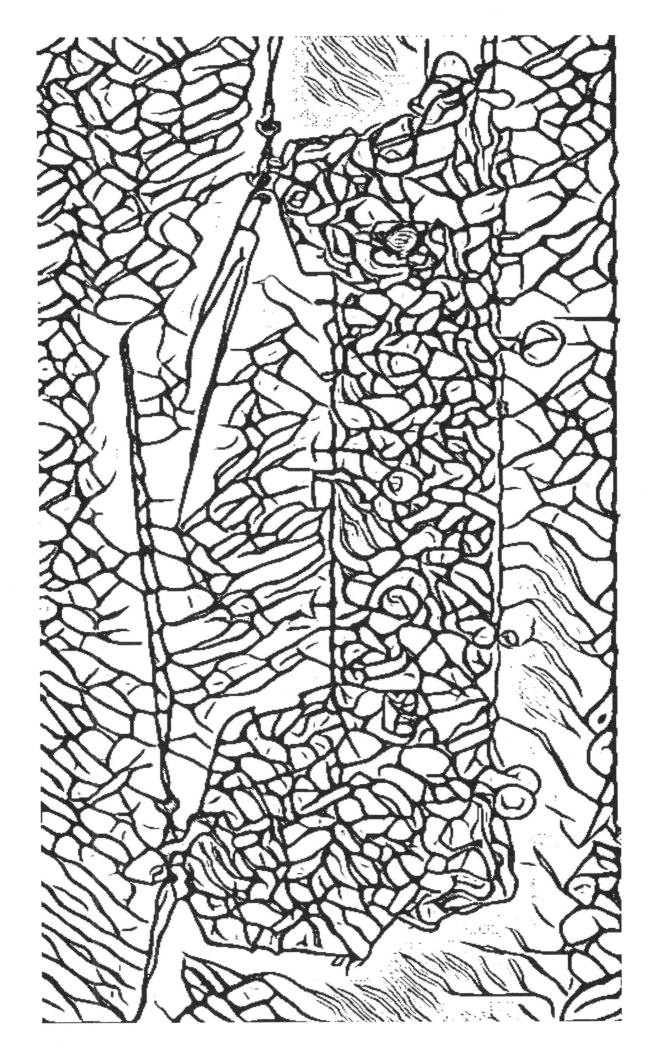

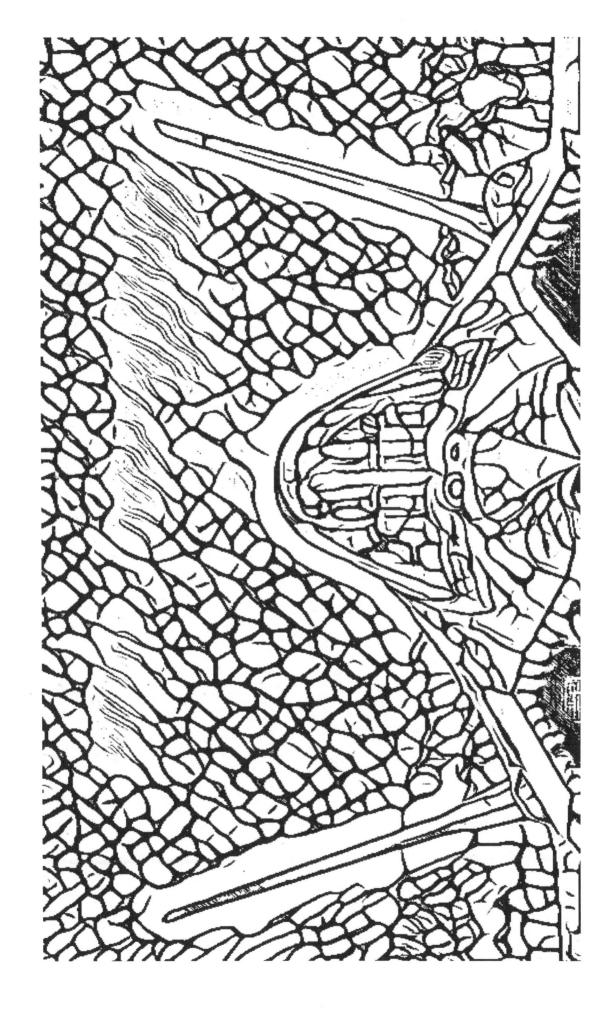

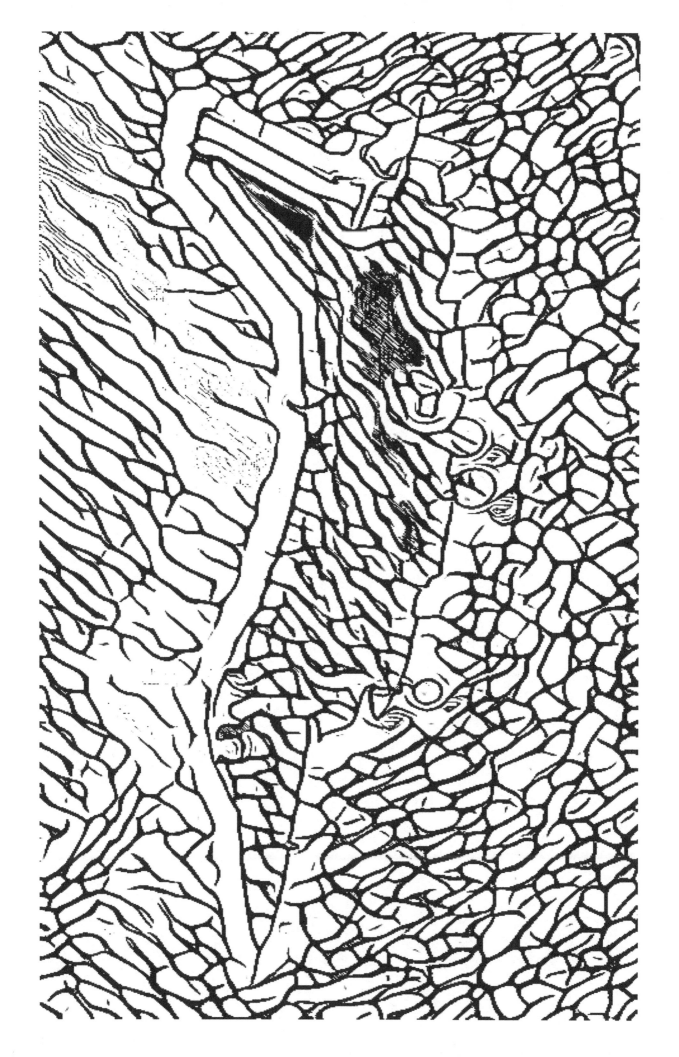

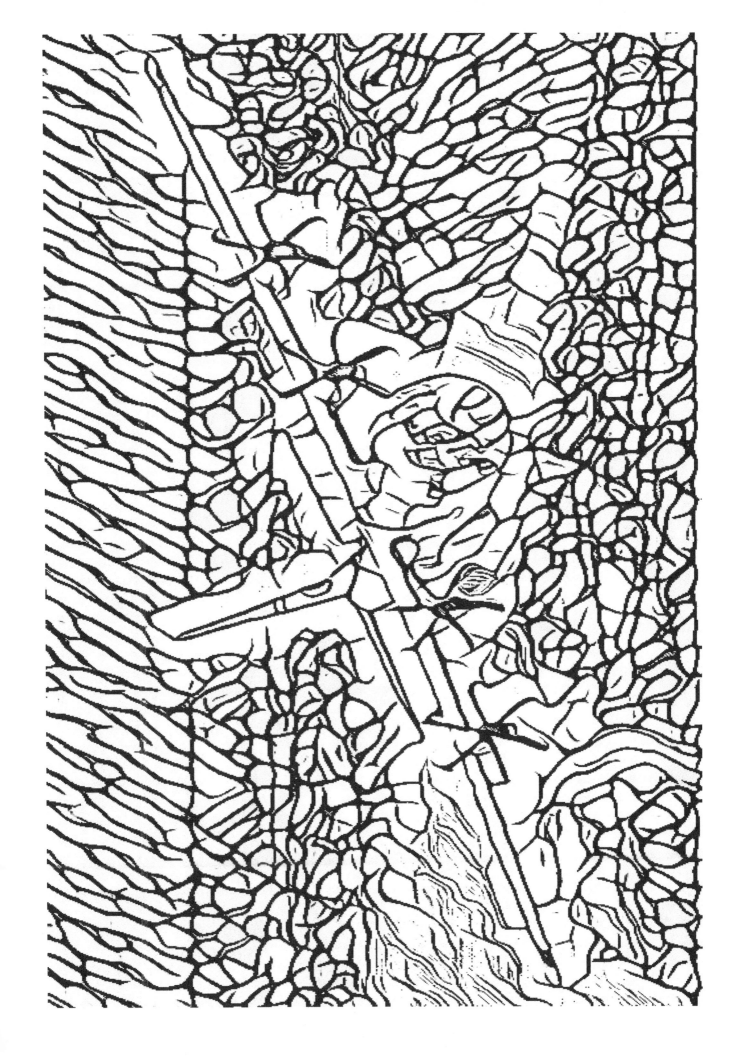

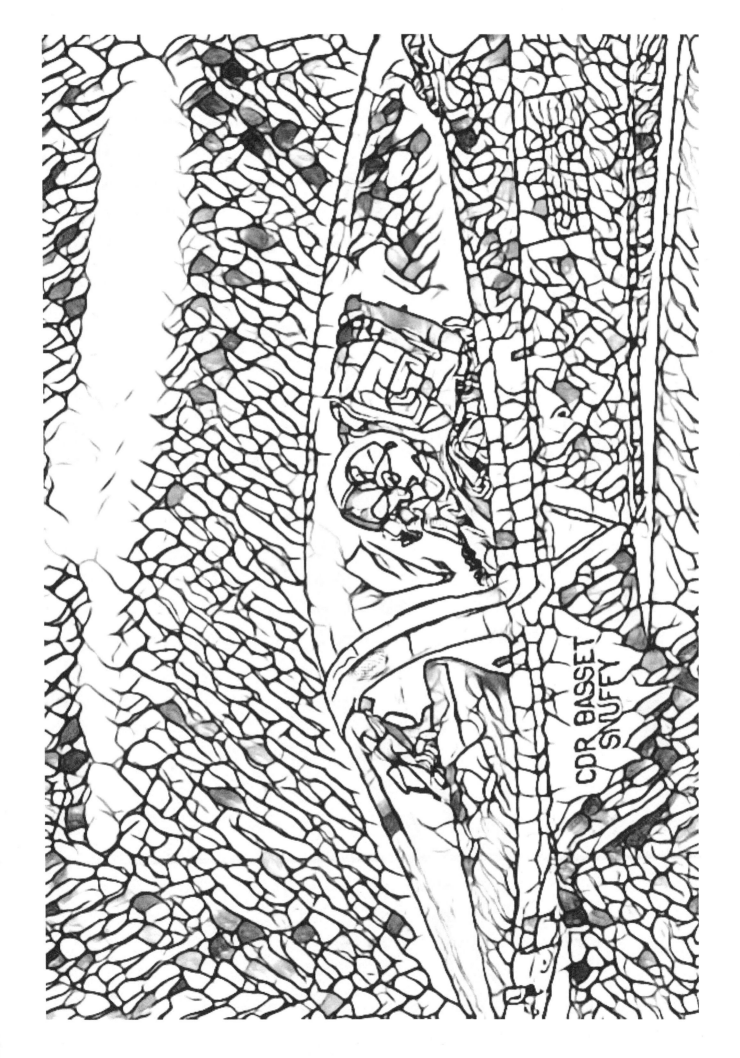

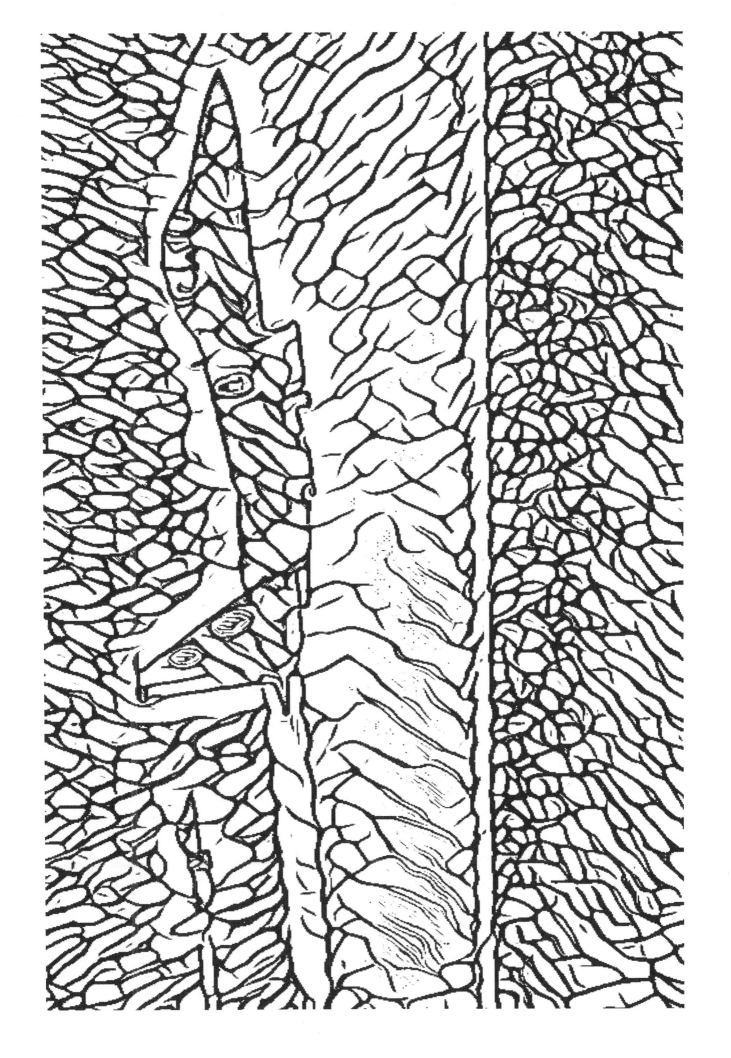

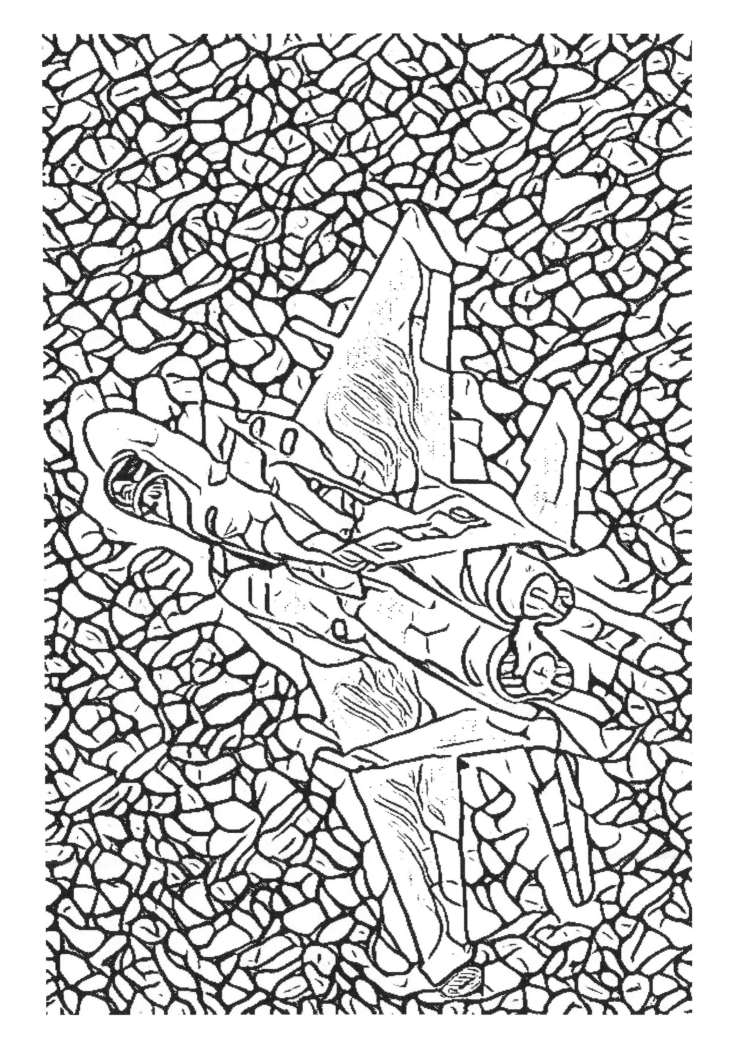

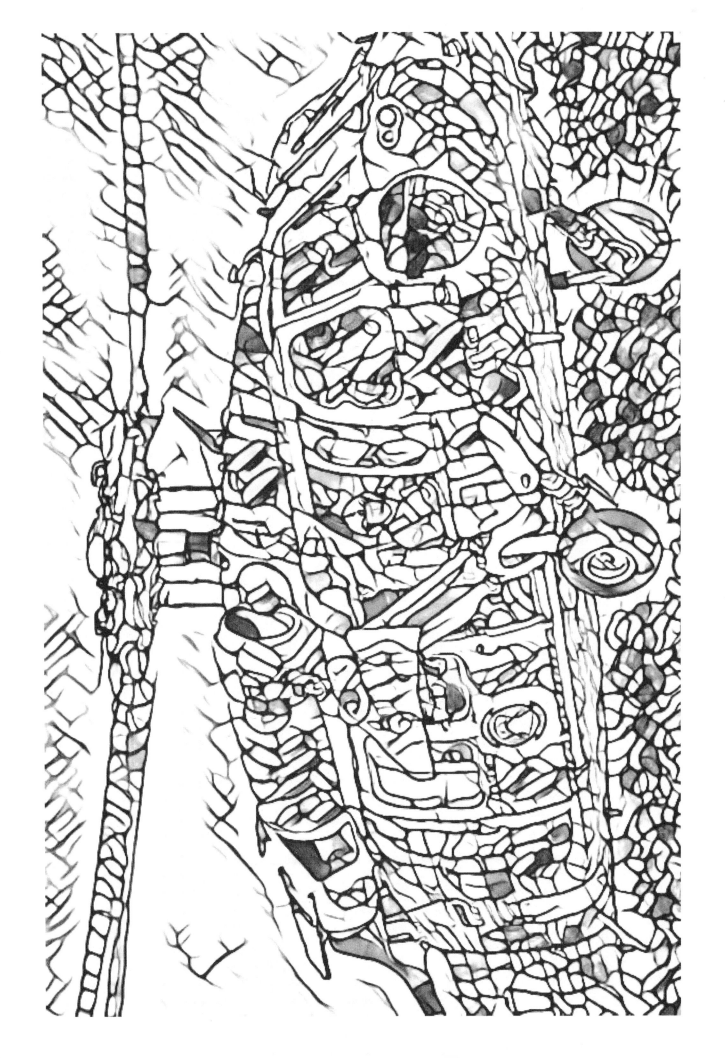

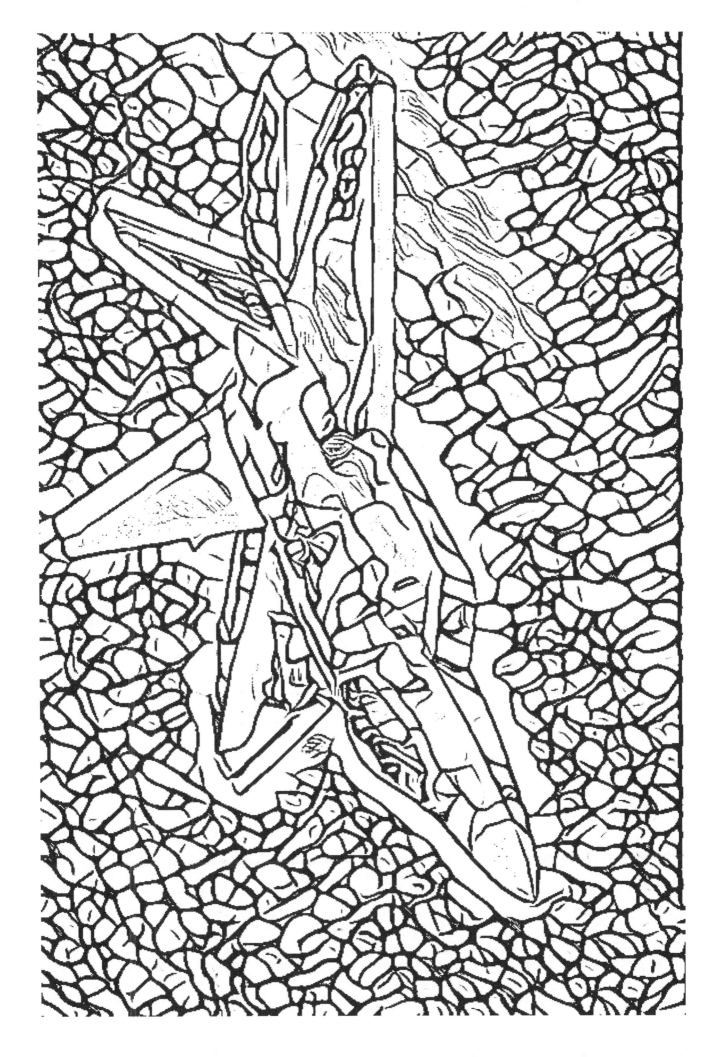

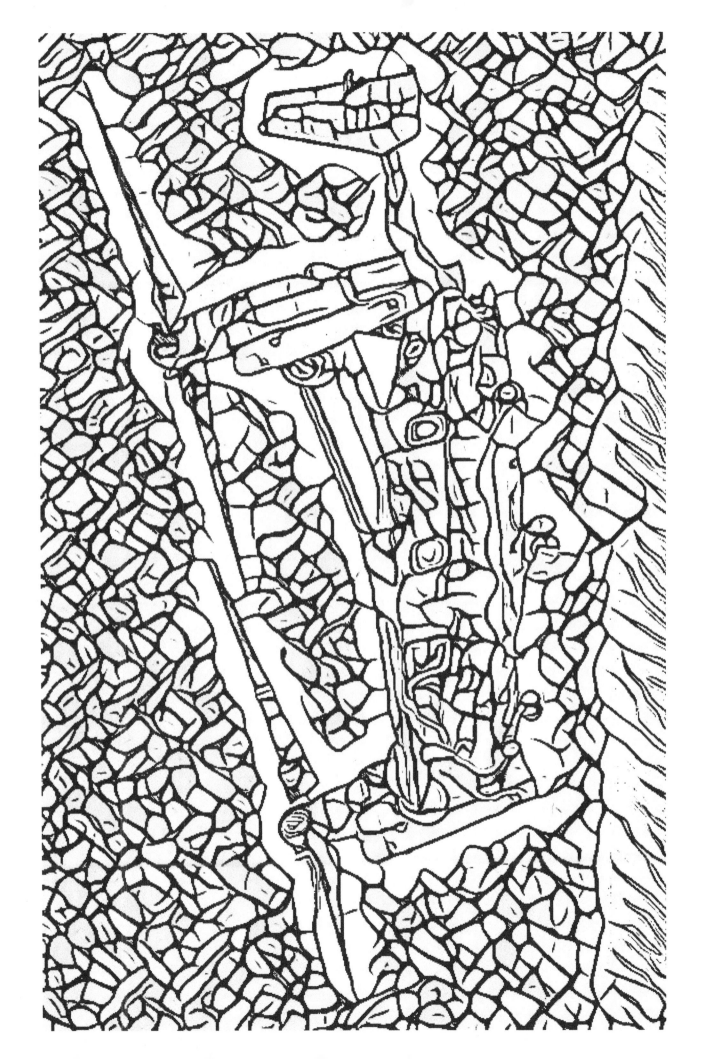

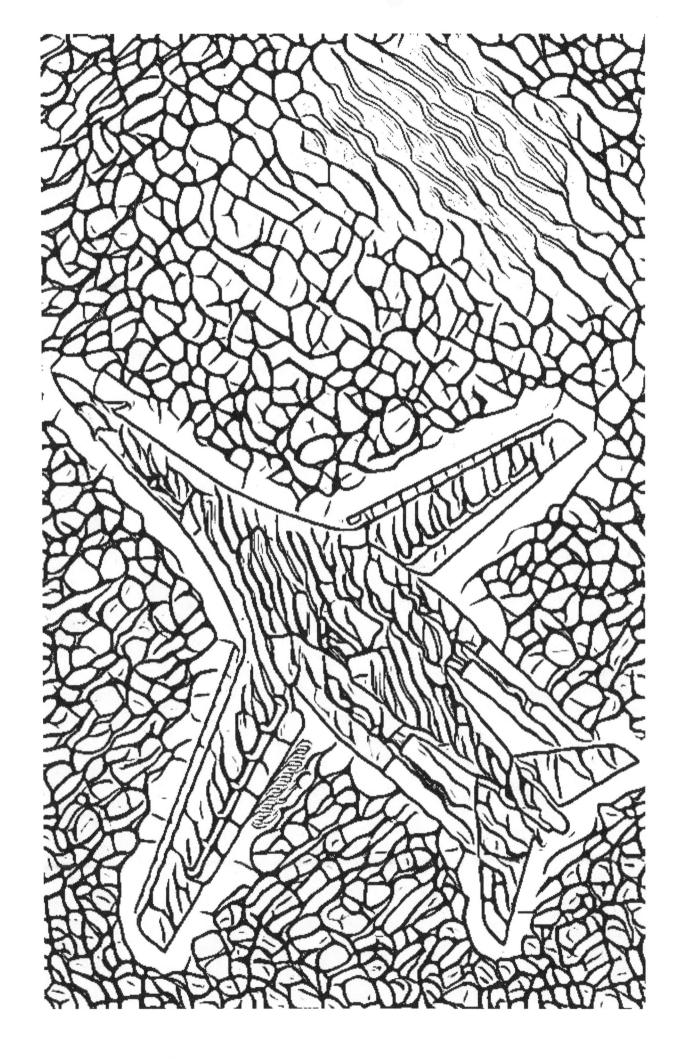

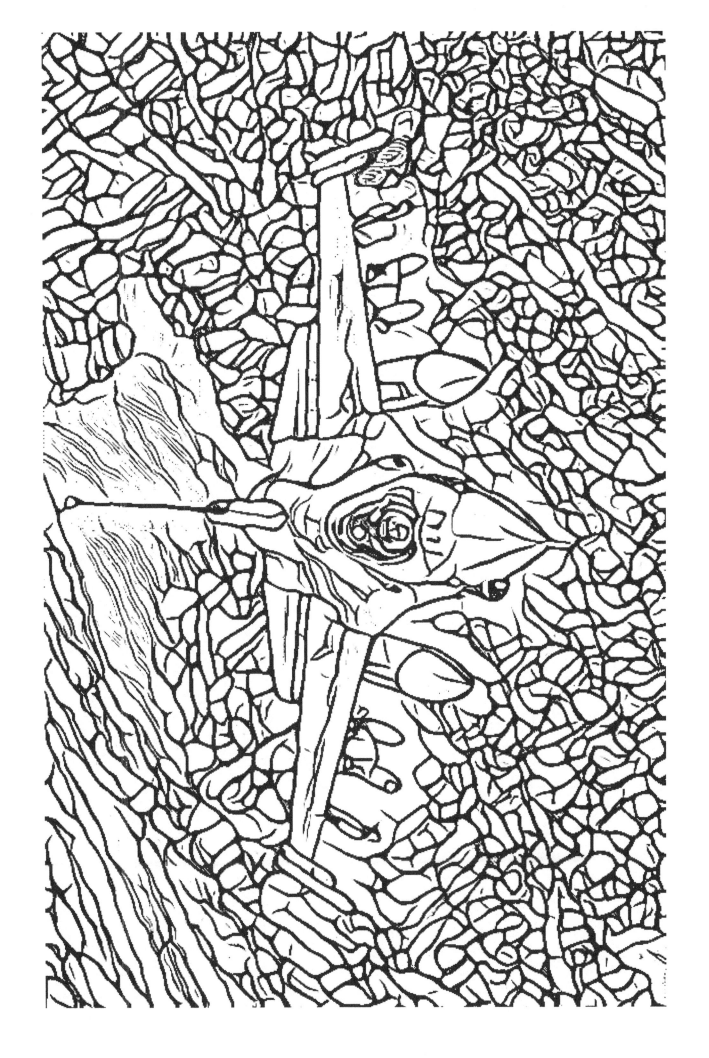

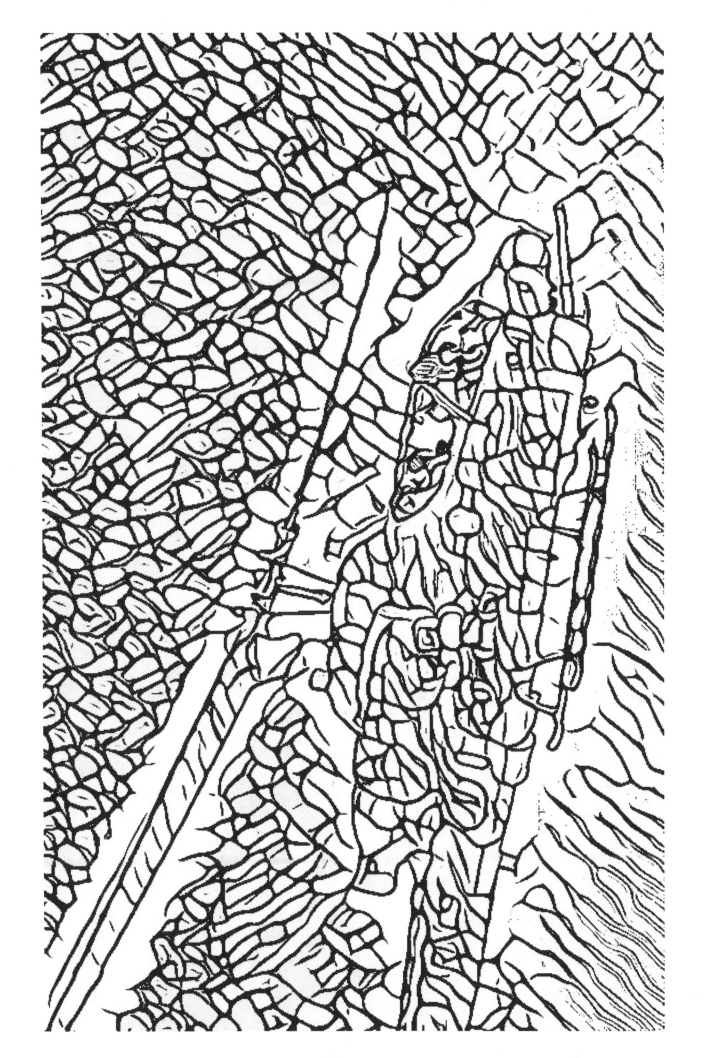

"Hitler built a fortress around Europe, but he forgot to put a roof on it."
President Franklin Roosevelt

Thank you for coloring this book.

Other Military Coloring Books For You:

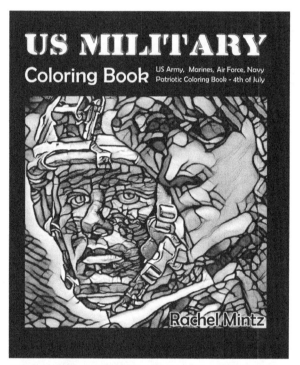

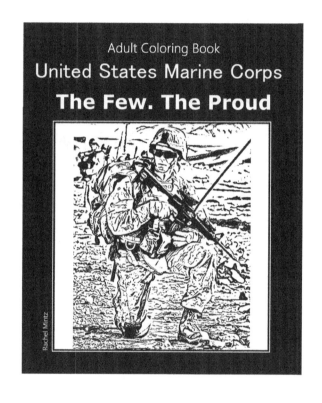

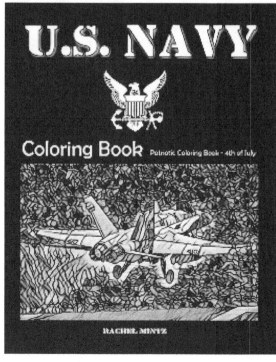

Coloring Books For Adults

US Military

Gorgeous Women Faces

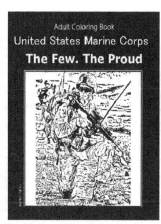

United States Marine Corps

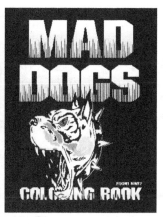

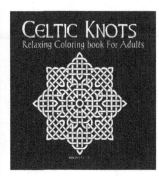

More Coloring Books For Kids

Flowers

Dogs

My First Patriotic

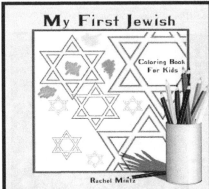

My First Jewish

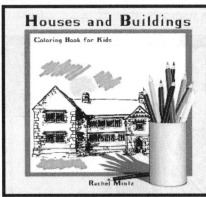

Houses and Buildings

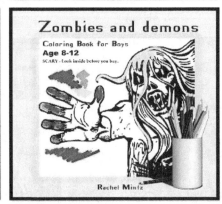

Zombies and demons

Toddler's Coloring Book

Pirates

Happy Cartoon Figures

Sports + Activity
Coloring Book
For Kids

Rachel Mintz

Space and Science
Coloring Book
For Kids

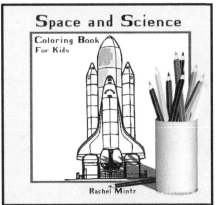

Rachel Mintz

Princesses Party
Coloring Book
For Girls

Rachel Mintz

Knights + Castles
Coloring Book
For Kids

Rachel Mintz

Cars
Coloring Book
for Kids

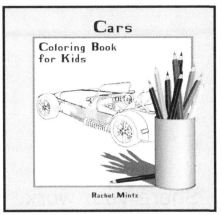

Rachel Mintz

Animals
Coloring Book
For Kids

Rachel Mintz

Guns and Rifles
Coloring Book
For Kids

Rachel Mintz

Army and Military
Coloring Book
For Kids

Rachel Mintz

Bible
Coloring Book For Kids

Rachel Mintz

Share your work.

Once you have colored few pages, how about to take some photos and add them as a review for this book at Amazon.

Made in the USA
Las Vegas, NV
14 November 2024

11819997R00059